# Short Family Walks on the Isle of Man

## (Sixteen round walks)

## John Kitto

**The Manx Experience**

*The Lady Isabella water wheel at Laxey*

# Contents

Published by
The Manx Experience, 45 Slieau Dhoo, Tromode Park, Douglas, Isle of Man.
Printed by Mannin Printing, Braddan, Isle of Man.

Maps by Ivan Sendall.   Photographs by John Kitto
Loghtan sheep drawings by SueWhite
(by kind permission of Peter Wade-Martins)

© John Kitto 1996

ISBN 1 873120 28 1

*Bound for Snaefell Summit*

# Introduction

The Isle of Man, surprisingly little known outside its traditional tourist catchment area in the north of England, is a walker's paradise. Within a total area of less than 230 square miles, it encompasses an amazing variety of scenery, from sand dunes and willowy marshes to remote heather-clad uplands, from deep wooded glens sheltering fast-flowing streams to open green pastures, from cliffs which plunge precipitately into the sea to sheltered bays with safe and gently shelving beaches.

It boasts hundreds of miles of well-signed footpaths, including four long-distance trails: the 90 mile *Raad ny Foillan* (Gull's Way in Manx Gaelic) which extends right round the entire coastline; the 22 mile Millennium Way which leads down the spine of the Island from Sky Hill near Ramsey in the north to Castletown, the old capital in the south; the 14 mile *Bayr ny Skeddan* (Herring Way) which follows a route across the hills from Peel to Castletown; and the Heritage Trail, along eleven miles of the former steam railway track from Douglas to Peel.

Those who are used to walking in the more popular areas of natural beauty in the United Kingdom will find that it is quite usual in the Island to walk for hours on the hills or in the glens without spotting an orange cagoule every few hundred yards or indeed seeing anyone at all. For that reason bird watchers and naturalists are always delighted with what the Island has to offer them.

As is often the case in holiday areas, the Isle of Man tends to shut down a number of facilities mentioned in the walks in this book during the winter, although the periods during which they remain closed vary considerably. For example, the Steam Railway service is wholly closed and the Electric Railway service is restricted.Below is a list of some of the other facilities affected.

Route 1   - Sound Cafe; Steam Railway museum; Cregneish Folk Museum.

Route 2   - Bradda Glen Café (bar remains open, but meals served at
            weekends only); Steam Railway museum.

Route 3   - Nautical Museum; Castle Rushen.

Route 4   - Boats from Port Erin to Calf of Man.

Route 5   - Silverdale boating lake.

Route 7   - Camera Obscura; Steam Railway.

Route 8   - Peel Castle.

Route 11  - Lady Isabella waterwheel.

Route 16  - Grove Rural Life Museum.

To ensure the facilities you require to see or use are open when visiting the Island during periods other than the summer season, it would be advisable to consult the Tourist Information Centre, Douglas (01624) 686766.

**Travel to the Isle of Man**

**By Air:** Manx Airlines (Central reservations linkline 01345 256256) operate direct flights to the Isle of Man from Belfast City*, Birmingham, Blackpool*, Cardiff, Cork*, Dublin, Glasgow, Jersey, Leeds/Bradford*, Liverpool, London Heathrow & Luton, Manchester, Newcastle*, and Southampton.

(* Operate in summer only).

Jersey European Airways (Central Reservations linkline 01345 676676) operate direct flights to the Isle of Man from Belfast City, Blackpool and Leeds/Bradford.

Emerald Airways (Reservations Liverpool 0151 448022) operate direct flights between Liverpool and the Isle of Man.

**By Sea:** The Isle of Man Steam Packet Co Ltd (Reservations 01624 661661) operates car ferries to Heysham, Fleetwood*†, Liverpool, Belfast*, and Dublin.

(* Operates in summer only)

(† Cars are not carried on this service).

Caledonian MacBrayne operates a ferry, summer only, between Ardrossan and the Isle of Man.

**Passports and Customs**

The Isle of Man is not, nor ever has been, a part of the United Kingdom. However, in line with the practice adopted for residents and visitors to and from Eire, those travelling between the UK and the Isle of Man as well as those travelling between Eire and the Isle of Man are not required to carry passports.

Thanks to a Customs Agreement between the UK and the Isle of Man by which the latter agrees to maintain the same rates of Excise Duty and VAT on non-exportable products as the UK, travellers between the UK and the Isle of Man will not pass through Customs at any time. This, however, does not apply to travellers between the Isle of Man and Eire, who will pass through Customs. Pets from the UK or Eire are not subject to quarantine regulations.

**When to come - and when not to!**

The Island is warmed by the waters of the Gulf Stream, whose mild winds still further moderate the climate, which is therefore temperate and lacking in extremes. The monthly average of sunshine hours is 130, the sunniest months being April, May and June when the monthly average is 210 hours. Rainfall is variable, depending on the locality, being least in the extreme south (760mm per annum). The driest months are March to June, and snowfall is infrequent. The highest recorded temperature is 27.8 degrees Centigrade and the lowest -11.9 degrees Centigrade. The average wind speed at Ronaldsway is 14.6 knots.

As one would expect, the Island tends to attract its share of holiday makers between May and September, but they usually stay in the main towns and seaside resorts. However, there are two periods which walkers should try to avoid. They are when the TT motorcycle races are held (usually in the last week in May and the first week in June, but check before coming) and when the Manx Grand Prix races are held (usually in the third and last weeks of August, but again check). The TT races in particular attract vast numbers of fans from all over the world and they bring their motorcycles with them. Not only are roads in the northern half of the Island closed for practices and races, but the fans themselves are let loose on the roads between races and are intimidating to say the least. There is also a shortage of short stay accommodation of every sort and restaurants and other public places tend to be crowded.

## Scenery and Character

The Isle of Man is effectively divided into two large upland masses, with Snaefell (2,036 ft) its only true mountain, dominating the northern section and South Barrule, legendary site of the summer palace of the sea god, Manannan MacLir, looming 1,586 ft over the south. A deep valley running south-west to north-east from Douglas via St Johns to Peel bisects the Island. The northern hills descend steeply to a low-lying triangular alluvial plain, while the southern hills slope away more gently down to a limestone bed around Castletown. The most dramatic cliff scenery is to be found down the west coast from Peel and all the way round the Sound to Port St Mary.

The heather covered uplands offer splendid views across to the surrounding countries in good weather. In fact, it is said that from the top of Snaefell six kingdoms are visible on a clear day: England, Scotland, Northern Ireland, Wales, Man - and the Kingdom of Heaven! The fells all belong to the Manx government and are open to ramblers. However, it has to be said that long treks across heather and sometimes bog are hard going for children and for this reason most of the walks in this book are coastal or run through one or more of the glens.

The Manx National Glens, as they are called, are essentially river valleys, varying in their character but in most cases deep, steep-sided clefts in the landscape, linking the hills with the sea and often containing waterfalls and dramatic rock formations. Seventeen of them are maintained by the Forestry Department and are provided with well-made paths, bridges, steps and hand rails where necessary, all in a natural unobtrusive style which makes them safe and pleasant to walk in without in any way spoiling their beauty. They too are open free of charge.

Most of the walks pass points of historical interest. Route 12, for instance, leads to Cashtal yn Ard, a funerary site dating back to around 1,800 BC. Above the waterfall at Spooyt Vane (Route 15) there are the remains of an early Christian keeil, a hermit's cell or chapel. Routes 3 and 8 to Castletown and Peel respectively take in the Island's two great castles. In Castle Rushen at Castletown (an excellent wet weather alternative; see page 21 ) can be seen one of the most perfectly preserved castles in Europe. Children will love the mediaeval figures which now inhabit it, complete with furnishings, sights and sounds of the past. Human habitation on St Patrick's Isle, where the ruins of Peel Castle and original cathedral stand, is now believed to date back some 5,000 years. The Heritage Centre in the town shows aspects of the Island's history and traditions.

Amongst the Island's other great attractions are its vintage transport systems. The Isle of Man Steam Railway runs between Douglas and Port Erin in the south-west. The Manx Electric Railway, which celebrated its centenary in 1993, runs northwards, between Douglas and Ramsey, with a branch line at Laxey climbing to the summit of Snaefell. Both operate with original rolling-stock in magnificent condition. There is a narrow-gauge steam railway at Groudle Glen, just north of Douglas, and in Douglas itself horse-drawn trams operate along the promenades all summer. There are also excellent country bus services - with modern vehicles!

The normal rules of enjoyable walking apply in the Isle of Man just as anywhere else: adequate clothing and, above all, sensible and waterproof footwear for all members are essential. In some cases, walking boots are called for. Parents may feel that some of the cliff-top walks (involved on Routes 1, 2, 8 and 13) are unsuitable for very young children or elderly people unsure of their footing.

It is taken for granted that readers of this book will be well aware of the Country Code and punctilious in keeping to its rules. These include keeping dogs strictly under control, especially important on the open fells of the Island where sheep graze freely, enclosed only by cattle grids on the approach roads.

A number of the walks suggested in this book include features specially chosen to appeal to children. For instance, there is a wonderful boating lake and playground with a water-driven roundabout at Silverdale Glen in Ballasalla (Route 5). There are also details of places for refreshments, where available.

The Manx Government publish a 1:25,000 map entitled 'Public Rights of Way and Outdoor Leisure Map'. This is being constantly updated and for all who propose walking in Man it would be a very worthwhile purchase. Stocks of maps are held in many Island stationers, at Government's Central Office in Douglas and at the Tourist & Events Information Centre, also in Douglas at the Sea Terminal.

## Routes in order of difficulty

*Starting with the easiest:*

| Route | 4 | Calf of Man | 2.5 miles | Route | 15 | Glen Wyllin | 4 miles |
|-------|----|-------------|-----------|-------|----|-------------|---------|
| Route | 16 | Ramsey | 2.5 miles | Route | 14 | Sulby | 2 miles |
| Route | 7 | Marine Drive | 4.5 miles | Route | 5 | Silverdale | 5.5 miles |
| Route | 3 | Castletown | 4 miles | Route | 8 | Peel | 3 miles |
| Route | 6 | St Johns | 3.5 miles | Route | 9 | Derbyhaven | 7 miles |
| Route | 11 | Laxey Wheel | 3 miles | Route | 2 | Bradda | 4 miles |
| Route | 13 | Maughold | 3.5 miles | Route | 10 | Baldwin Valley | 7 miles |
| Route | 12 | Ballaglass | 4.5 miles | Route | 1 | Cregneish | 7 miles |

# Wet Weather Alternatives during the Summer

**Douglas:**

**Crescent Leisure Centre, Central Promenade.** Tel: (01624) 676207. Game machines; dodgems; wax museum.

**Derby Castle Aquadrome, King Edward Road.** Tel: (01624) 673411. Two heated indoor swimming pools; water massage spa baths; sauna cabin; Russian and Turkish steam rooms; cold plunge; sunbeds.

**Gaiety Theatre, Harris Promenade.** Tel: (01624) 625001. Live theatrical productions.

**Manx Museum & National Heritage, corner of Kingswood Grove and Crellins Hill.** Tel: (01624) 675522. An award-winning museum which will interest children as well as adults.

**Manx Superbowl, Castle Mona Hotel, Central Promenade.** Tel: (01624) 612020. Indoor bowling (ten pin); bar; restaurant.

**Murrays Motorcycle Museum, The Bungalow, Snaefell.** Historic motorcycles and other memorabilia.

**National Sports Centre, New Castletown Road (Quarterbridge).Tel: (01624) 611553.** Opening October 1997, 25m pool, leisure lagoon with two flume rides

**Nautilus Fitness Centre, 21 Strand Street.** Tel: (01624) 626368. Gymnasium and keep fit centre.

**Palace Cinema, Central Promenade.** Tel: (01624) 676814. Two screens.

**Paramount City Night Club, The Crescent, Queens Promenade.** Tel: (01624) 622447 Disco entertainment.

**Piazza Cinema, in Summerland** qv below.

**Summerland Sports & Leisure Centre, King Edward Road.** Tel: (01624) 662551. Children's play area; roller skating; squash; badminton; table tennis; gymnasium; sunbeds; sauna; Cave Disco; cinema.

**Villa Marina Concert Hall, Harris Promenade.** Tel: (01624) 628855. Live variety and sporting entertainment.

**Ramsey:**

**Grove Rural Life Museum, Bowring Road.** Tel: (01624) 675522. A time capsule Victorian period house, the rooms, from drawing room to scullery, retain their period furnishings. Beautifully maintained gardens. Displays of toys, costumes.

**Lucky Star Amusement Centre, Market Place.** Tel: (01624) 812283. Games machines.

**Nightlife Disco, Saddle Hotel, Market Square.** Tel: (01624) 812283.

**Port Erin:**

**Beachcomber Amusements, South Parade.** Tel: (01624) 832977. Games machines.

**Steam Railway Museum, Station Road.** Historic locomotives, rolling stock and other railway memorabilia.

**Castletown:**

**Castle Rushen.** Tel: (01624) 823326. Beautifully preserved mediaeval castle with figures, furnishings, sights and sounds of the past.

**Nautical Museum, Bridge Street.** Tel: (01624) 675522. The Island's sea-going history. Contains 18th century armed yacht, replica sail maker's loft and stern cabin of a ship of the Nelson period.

**Old Grammar School,** near the main car park. Built around 1200 AD as the Island capital's first church, but also played an important role in the history of Manx education.

**Peel:**

**The Heritage Centre** incorporates displays of the Island's early Celtic inhabitants, its Viking political and artistic culture, and its maritime tradition.

**St Johns:**

**Tynwald Craft Centre.** Tel: (01624) 801213. A collection of craft shops and a restaurant centred on a tweed manufacturing mill.

# Map Key

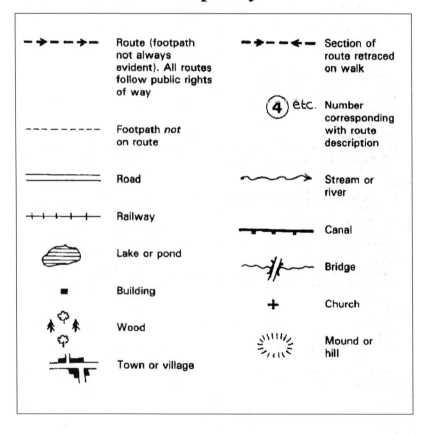

| | |
|---|---|
| **➤ — ➤ —** | Route (footpath not always evident). All routes follow public rights of way |
| **- - - - - - -** | Footpath *not* on route |
| ═══════ | Road |
| ┼┼┼┼┼ | Railway |
| | Lake or pond |
| ■ | Building |
| | Wood |
| | Town or village |
| **➤ — ◄ —** | Section of route retraced on walk |
| **④** etc. | Number corresponding with route description |
| ～～～➤ | Stream or river |
| | Canal |
| | Bridge |
| ✛ | Church |
| | Mound or hill |

*The Steam Railway museum at Port Erin.*

*Wool spinning at Cregneish.*

# ROUTE 1 7 miles
## Cregneish

**Outline**

The Sound - Port Erin Marine Biological Station - Steam Railway Museum - Ballnahowe - Mull Hill - Cregneish Folk Museum - The Chasms - Spanish Head - The Sound

**Summary**

The first part of this walk is above the cliffs along the south-west coast of the Island to Port Erin. On the return trip, a part is inland and the final section is once again along the cliff tops, but on the south coast. Although only seven miles in length, this is a strenuous walk with some fairly stiff climbs. It is desirable to allow 1.5 hours to Port Erin and 2 hours for the return trip, apart from time spent at the museum or elsewhere. Walking boots are essential.

**Attractions**

The Sound is the name given to the stretch of water between the Island and two small islets, the larger of which is called the Calf of Man (see Route 4). The 'lands end' part of the Island has thus come to be referred to as the Sound. The coastal path to Port Erin along the cliff tops provides the walker with striking scenery, but does not come close enough to the edge to cause vertigo. The cliffs make good breeding grounds for birds, and bird watchers should bring binoculars. Apart from the variety of sea birds, they may see peregrines and the black-bodied chough, which has red legs and red beak.

The black conical buoy which is located at the entrance to Port Erin bay some way out from the shore marks the seaward end of a ruined breakwater which the Manx government arranged to have built across the bay in 1864. Its purpose, so it was said, was 'to provide protection in bad weather to ships of the Royal Navy'. In fact, it was wanted for the benefit of Manx fishing boats. Having borrowed a huge sum of money from the British government, the breakwater was built, but in 1884 an unusually severe storm demolished it. The British government never got their money back!

The attractive small harbour in the port is where boats to the Calf of Man sail from (see Route 4). The beach is one of the best in the Island, composed of fine golden sand and shelving so gently that bathing is safe for the smallest of children.

The Steam Railway Museum will be a haven for steam buffs. It houses early locomotives and carriages as well as models and much other memorabilia.

On the Mull Hill south of Port Erin there is the Mull Circle, unique in the British Isles. It is a megalithic stone circle and consists of six pairs of burial chambers. The Hill itself (556 ft) is the site of the southernmost civilisation on the Island, once farmed by Neolithic Picts. *(Continued on page 15)*

**11**

# Route 1

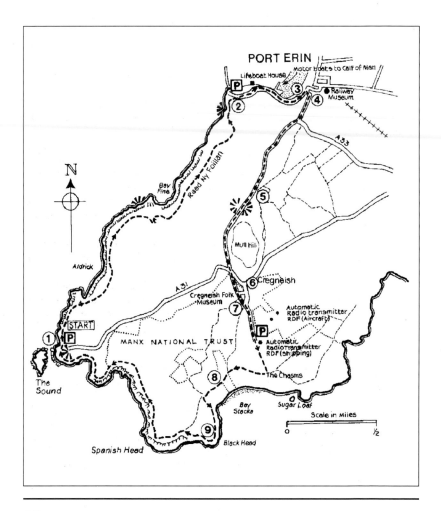

# ROUTE 1 7 miles
## Cregneish

**Start**

*The Sound is about 2.5 miles west of Port St Mary and has a good-sized car park which is free. OS Sheet No 95 (GR 174667).*

**Route**

1. *The walk starts at the stile to the west of the Sound Café and continues along the top of the high cliffs. The track is rough in places, but should pose no difficulty for any normally fit child or adult.*

2. *The route is well marked and descends towards Port Erin bay through two rusty kissing gates, joining the bayside road from behind the buildings of the Marine Biological Station. Turn right along the road, passing the lifeboat station and harbour jetty on the left. (There are public toilets opposite the jetty).*

3. *Follow the road around the beach and to the right (Strand Road) as it climbs towards the town centre. Turn first left and then right into Station Road. The Steam Railway Museum is on the corner on the right.*

4. *Retrace your steps back along Strand Road, but instead of turning right towards the beach carry straight on along Glen View Road, St George's Crescent and into Ballafurt Road. Turn left on entering Ballafurt Road and walk straight on to a narrow lane which climbs steeply. This is Ballnahowe Road.*

5. *After the stiff climb, the road levels out and on the skyline ahead and to the left can be seen the fencing around the Mull Circle. A stile allows entry into the site on Mull Hill.*

6. *At the end of Ballnahowe Road, cross over the Port St Mary to the Sound road to get into the Cregneish Village Folk Museum. A short cut back to the Sound can be made by turning right at this point.*

7. *Leave Cregneish by the road leading southwards towards the Chasms which lie on the coast ahead. At two points along this road there are footpath signs on the right to indicate slightly shorter routes back to the Sound. However, to complete the full walk - and to view the Chasms if desired - walk past the small building on the left at the end of the road, climb over the stile and walk on down to the coast, where you should turn right. (Turn left for the Chasms).*

8. *The footpath runs around Bay Stacka, at the far end of which one can look across to the opposite end of the bay and see the tall spike of rock known as the Sugar Loaf.*

9. *The path keeps fairly close to the tall cliffs of Black Head and Spanish Head, but, providing normal good sense is displayed, there is no danger of walking over the edge at any time. Soon after leaving Spanish Head, the Sound Café with its whirling aero-generator and car park can be seen below. Care, however, should be taken not to slip on the rough descent between the Head and the Sound.*

*Cregneish Folk Museum display of Manx dancing.*

*Port Erin Harbour where boats leave for the Calf of Man.*

*(Continued from page 11)*

The Cregneish Village Folk Museum is a unique illustration of 19th century life in a Manx upland crofting community. The whitewashed and thatched buildings house a weaver's shed, a turner's workshop or smithy, and Harry Kelly's cottage, a typical Manx homestead furnished in the style of the period. A herd of the rare Loghtan sheep with their four-horned heads is usually to be seen grazing nearby.

A sight which might give the walker the impression of an encounter with a flying saucer can be seen on high ground to the east and south of the village. This strange circular edifice which looks as though it is about to make a vertical take-off is in fact a radio direction finding beacon for aircraft landing at the Island's airport near Castletown.

The Chasms lie 200 to 300 yards to the left of the route of this walk and where small children are involved it may be wise not to make the necessary detour to visit the area. They consist of a number of deep vertical cracks in the rock face. Providing one looks where one is walking they pose no danger and in high summer are ablaze with colour from the rock plants which have established themselves there.

*The Sound from the Calf of Man.*

**Refreshments**

At the Sound Café and at various restaurants, snack bars and public houses in Port Erin.

**Public transport**

By bus: Douglas Bus Station; service No 1A and 3A.

By steam train: Douglas Steam Railway Station to Port Erin Station. Start and finish the walk from the Steam Railway Museum.

*The Milner Tower at Bradda Head.*

# ROUTE 2      4 miles
## Bradda

**Outline**
Bradda Glen - Bradda Head - Fleshwick - Bradda East - Bradda Glen

**Summary**
This is a coastal walk with spectacular views of the south coast, the Calf of Man and the north-west coast of the Island, with the Mull of Galloway beyond. Walking boots essential.

**Attractions**
This is a good opportunity to visit the Steam Railway Museum in Port Erin before or after this walk. It is on the corner of Station Road and Strand Road.

From Bradda Glen where this walk begins, there is an attractive path along the north shore of the beautiful bay of Port Erin up to the Milner Tower, the oddly-shaped castle-like edifice standing on top of Bradda Head.

Born in 1804, William Milner was a partner in his father's firm manufacturing fire-resistant safes. When his health began to deteriorate, he spent many holidays in Port Erin and eventually retired to live there. He was a God-fearing man who befriended the inhabitants, providing sustenance to the old and clothing the poor children of the village. He was also the prime instigator of the breakwater across the bay whose ruins can still be seen between the black conical buoy, sitting in the middle of the bay, and the south shore. (See Route 1 for details).

Seldom does a man live to see a monument erected to him, but, such was Milner's charisma, in 1871 the Milner Tower was built in the shape of a Milner safe key. The money was raised by public subscription and Milner was so delighted that he provided a substantial sum himself! He died three years later.

The tower can be entered and steps lead to a fine look-out spot where the Island to the south-west and much of the Calf of Man can be seen. (See Route 4 for Calf of Man).

Fleshwick is a small attractive cove about 500 yards to the left of the route of this walk and is worth making a detour to see it. Like all Island names ending in 'wick', it signifies that the name was given to the inlet by the Vik-ings, ie, those Scandinavian warriors who were driven from their native viks (creeks or fiords) and eventually settled down and ruled the Island for roughly 300 years.

**Refreshments**
From the car park facing the bay in Bradda Glen, the path to the left leads to a public house/café and toilets. There are tables and benches on the lawn in front of the building for sitting out and admiring the view in good weather.

**Public transport**
By bus: Douglas Bus Station, service Nos 1, 1A, 2, 2A. Alight in Bridson Road, walk up the Promenade to Bradda Glen.

By train: Douglas Steam Railway Station to Port Erin. Walk up the Promenade to Bradda Glen.

# Route 2

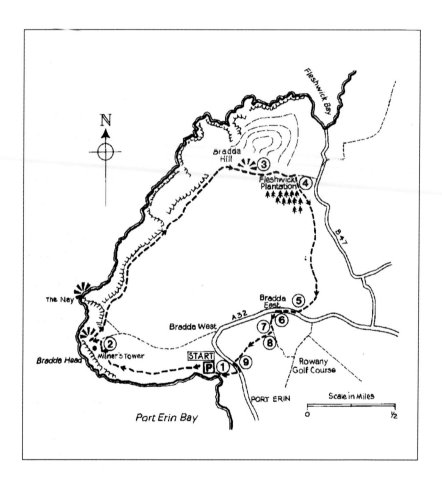

# ROUTE 2
## Bradda
**4 miles**

**Start**

*At Bradda Glen. From Douglas, take the A5 road to Port Erin. Upon entering the shopping area, the one-way street leads to the Promenade. Continue up the Promenade to Bradda Road and turn left at the signpost indicating Bradda Glen. There is a free car park facing Port Erin bay in the glen. OS Sheet 95 (GR 193697).*

**Route**

1. *Leaving the car park, walk towards the bay ahead and turn right on to the coastal footpath running beside the bay. Turn right again when it ends and walk up to the Milner Tower. This is quite a steep but short, rocky climb.*

2. *After leaving the tower, head northwards, keeping to the path which runs along the cliff tops. Climb over the stile, following the well-defined path up to the highest part of the walk, 726 ft above the sea. This climb is quite arduous, but is split into four parts - the second is the hardest - with flat and even small downhill stretches of ground between the uphill climbs. You will know you have reached the end of the climb when a cairn is visible on the right.*

3. *The path now begins to slope downhill, becoming increasingly steep, but should cause no problem if tackled with reasonable care by well shod walkers. As you near the end of the descent, you will see a part of Fleshwick cove on the left and a white kissing gate ahead which leads into a field. (If you wish to take a rest or have a picnic at Fleshwick, go through the gate, down the field beyond and turn left on to the road. Upon leaving Fleshwick afterwards, walk up the road until you see a footpath sign on the right. This leads through the yard of the Ballaglonney Farm, making a right-angled turn to the left between farm buildings and on to the track along the edge of the Fleshwick plantation).*

4. *If you wish to continue the walk without a detour to Fleshwick, turn on to the small footpath to the right before going through the white gate. This leads on to the track along the edge of Fleshwick plantation.*

5. *The track ends soon after it turns sharply to the right, debouching on to a narrow road. Keep straight ahead on this road as it rises gently, with a golf course on its left and houses on its right.*

6. *As you reach the crest of the rise, look out for a footpath sign on the left. The ladderstile here is not very easy to see, so you should keep a keen look-out for the sign.*

7. *Climb over the stile and walk diagonally to the right hand bottom corner of the field to which it gives access. There is a rather interesting form of chain link exit from the field; just pull the two centre metal uprights apart.*

8. *You will be at the edge of the golf course. Turn right as indicated by the sign and stick to the right side of the course until you reach a green which sits above you on the left. At this point you will see a narrow footpath to the right which joins a road with a red telephone box at the juncture.*

9. *Turn left and cross the road. You will see the pedestrian entrance to Bradda Glen beneath a stone arch well marked as such.*

*Castle Rushen and Castletown harbour.*

# ROUTE 3        4 miles
## Castletown

**Outline**

Castletown - Scarlett - Poyllvaaish - Witches Mill - Nautical Museum - Castle Rushen - Castletown

**Summary**

About a half of this walk is along a coastal path west of Castletown. Thereafter the path turns inland and approaches the town from the north-east. The whole walk is on the flat and ordinary outdoor shoes can be worn.

**Attractions**

Still the most picturesque of all the Manx towns, Castletown was the Island's capital until 1869 when it lost that title to Douglas, due to the shallowness of the water in Castletown Bay and the smallness of its harbour.

Nowadays, the harbour mainly shelters yachts and other pleasure craft and is dominated by the imposing battlements of Castle Rushen. The castle is one of the best preserved in Europe. It has its origins in the Norse period and the last Viking King of Man, Magnus, died there in 1265. The settlement which grew up to serve the castle and its garrisons became the main government centre until Douglas took over.

As the fortress of the kings and lords of Man, Castle Rushen now houses some spectacular recreated displays of life in the mediaeval and 17th century periods. Parts of the building are still used as court rooms and the swearing-in ceremony for each successive Lieutenant-Governor of the Island - an appointment made by the British monarch - takes place here.

It was badly damaged during the siege of Robert Bruce in 1313, restored and enlarged between 1343 and 1345, and was captured by Cromwell's general, Lord Fairfax, in 1652. The south tower has a one-handed clock reputed to have been presented by Queen Elizabeth I in 1597 when she held the Island.

On the opposite side of the harbour to the castle, and a few yards along Bridge Street, there is the Nautical Museum which contains an 18th century armed yacht, 'The Peggy', built by a Manxman in 1791. She lies in her original boathouse where she remained undisturbed for a century after her owner's death, being rediscovered in 1935. A replica sail maker's loft, ship models, other exhibits and photographs bring alive Manx maritime life and trade in the days of sail, including a replica stern cabin of a ship of the Nelson period.

Between the car park (for location see **Start**) and the outer harbour, there is the old Grammar School. Built around 1200 AD as the Island's first church, St Mary's Chapel also played an important role in the history of Manx education. A school was first recorded in the chapel in 1570 and from 1702, when a new church was built, served exclusively in that capacity until its closure in 1930. Its displays recount its varied history. *(Continued on page 24)*

# Route 3

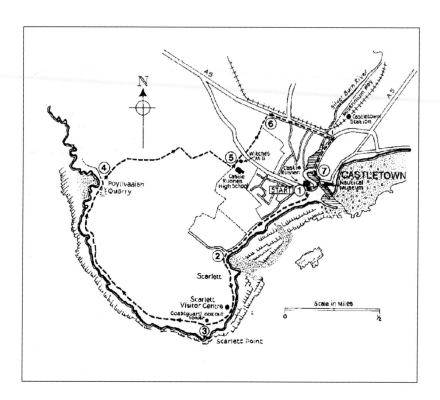

# ROUTE 3                                    4 miles
## Castletown

**Start**

*At the car park which lies on the seaward side of Castletown Police Station, Post Office and the town's central square called The Parade. OS Sheet 95 (GR 265675).*

**Route**

*1. Leave the car park at its western exit which leads into the main square (The Parade). Turn left and keep to the road as it leads past small fishermen's cottages along the shore.*

*2. The road bends to the left, following the shore line to Scarlett (Cormorant cleft) Point, where there is a Visitors' Centre.*

*3. As the now disused Coastguard look-out tower is passed, the Chicken Rock lighthouse comes into view ahead and to the south of the Calf of Man islet.*

*4. A green shed and the workings of the Poyllvaaish quarry will be recognised by a number of slabs of polished marble awaiting transport which are lying around. About 200 yards after passing the shed, twin tubular metal gates appear on your right. Just beyond the second one, there is a stone stile. Climb over this and head straight out across the field. At the far side, there are two wooden farm gates, although the right hand one is usually kept open. Go through the right one and thereafter follow the green finger posts and ladder stile which will lead you to the Castle Rushen High School and the Witches' Mill tower.*

*5. Turn left into a short lane which quickly debouches on to a metalled road. Cross this road and take the lane almost opposite. It leads between houses and seemingly almost into private gardens, but persevere until it comes to an end. The main Castletown to Port St Mary road is now ahead. Turn right and walk along it.*

*6. Keep to the right hand pavement as this is quite a busy road, turning right beside the Silverburn River at the first roundabout.*

*7. Do not cross the harbour by the road bridge. Instead, continue along Bridge Street until the sign indicating the Nautical Museum is visible. Before reaching it, you will see a metal footbridge across the narrow 'throat' of the harbour. Use the bridge to get to the front entrance of Castle Rushen, should you wish to view it, and back to the car park.*

*(Continued from page 21)*

In the town's central square, called The Parade, as it used to serve as the parade ground for Castle Rushen's military garrison, is a Doric column on a plinth. This was erected in 1836 in memory of a General Cornelius Smelt, the Island's Lt-Governor between 1805 and 1832. The people of Castletown refused to contribute towards the cost of a statue of him on top of the column, so it has remained just a column to this day.

Poyllvaaish (Death Pool, although in fact it is a small bay), past which this walk goes, contains only a marble quarry. It yields a black limestone which works down into a very smooth surface and can be varnished. In appearance it is a good copy at first of black Derbyshire limestone. However, it does not last when exposed to the elements and becomes pock-marked. That the steps of St Paul's Cathedral were made of this stone is proudly recorded as a result of what Richard Townley wrote in his 'Journal kept in the Isle of Man' in 1791. But its veracity is suspect to put it mildly!

The round tower near Castle Rushen High School, which is passed towards the end of this walk, is still known as the Witches' Mill, although that name is no longer justified. During the 1950s, a Mr G B Gardner, the owner of a unique collection of occult items, converted the three-storey limestone barn adjoining the tower into a museum of witchcraft and magic. However, the whole collection was subsequently sold to the 'Ripley - believe it or not' organisation in the United States.

**Refreshments**

Available in public houses, cafés and restaurants in Castletown.

**Public Transport**

By bus: From Douglas Bus Station, service Nos 1, 1A, 1C.
By train: From Douglas Steam Railway Station.

*Lifelike figures dining at Castle Rushen.*

# ROUTE 4  2.5 miles
## The Calf of Man

**Outline**

Port Erin - Calf of Man - Port Erin

**Summary**

This is more of a ramble than a walk to a set route, with a sea trip from Port Erin to the Calf of Man to start off with. The boat trip takes about half an hour and waterproofs should be taken to guard against spray. Landing from and getting aboard boats make this walk unsuitable for the very young or the infirm. Walking shoes will suffice in dry weather, otherwise walking boots should be worn.

**Attractions**

Given good weather, the boat trip itself should prove a thoroughly enjoyable experience to all except those very prone to seasickness. However, the latter can always be in the open air and as small boats do not roll and pitch like larger vessels, it is unlikely that the short trip will cause more than temporary queasiness.

The Calf of Man is a bird sanctuary and there are usually two bird wardens staying at the only farmhouse on it, where they net, ring and record the bird population. (Bona fide ornithologists can obtain a permit from the Manx Museum, telephone (01624) 675522, to stay a few days at the house). The variety of land and sea birds on the islet adds immensely to the enjoyment of spending even a few hours on this wild and pretty spot, and grey seals can often be seen basking on the rocks or feeding offshore. The best time to visit the Calf is in May when the birds are nesting on the cliffs and the islet is carpeted with bluebells, pinks and even late-flowering primroses.

There are good tracks leading from the normal landing place on the north coast to the south and, as the islet is only about one mile square, it is difficult to get lost.

The most striking man-made sight on the islet is the three lighthouse towers at its southern tip. In 1815, an Act of Parliament brought the Isle of Man under the jurisdiction of the Northern Lighthouses Board, which was and still is responsible for security of navigation in the northern parts of the British Isles, just as Trinity House is responsible for England, Wales, the Channel Isles and Gibraltar. Robert Stevenson, who was appointed Engineer to the Northern Lighthouses Board in 1797 and served in that capacity for 45 years, erected at least 15 major lights, including two of the three on the Calf, both built in 1818. The two towers were placed so that they would line up on the dreaded Chicken Rock reef, but in fog or low cloud they proved useless and in 1874 it was decided to build another lighthouse, this time on the reef itself. That can be seen out to sea south of the Calf and was built by Robert's son, Thomas (the father of Robert Louis Stevenson) and his brother, David. After a disastrous fire in 1960 on the Chicken Rock lighthouse, it was converted to automatic
*(Continued on page 29)*

## Route 4

# ROUTE 4                                   2.5 miles

## The Calf of Man

**Start**

*Motor fishing boats leave from the harbour at Port Erin (OS Sheet 95, GR 194689) for the Calf between Easter and September, weather permitting.*

**Route**

*From the small rocky landing spot on the Calf, follow the main track south. This passes the farmhouse which accommodates the bird wardens and ends at the south-western coast where the lighthouses stand.*

*There are other tracks and paths which will take the rambler to the south-east coast, where there is a small landing place called South Harbour. Apart from keeping clear of cliff edges and making certain they are back at the boat pick-up point at the time agreed, the family members should feel free to wander wherever their fancy takes them. If any children wish to go to the extreme southern point of the islet from South Harbour, they should be accompanied by an adult.*

**Notice at Port Erin harbour for boats to the Calf of Man. (1996 prices!)**

*One of the wardens at the Calf of Man bird sanctuary.*

*The Calf lighthouses with Chicken Rock in the distance. The newer light on the Calf is between the two towers.*

*(Continued from page 25)*

operation. A third and more powerful lighthouse and fog signal was constructed on the Calf between the two old towers. Inaugurated in 1968 and now also converted to automatic operation, the new building stands 312 ft above sea level, has a light of two million candlepower from an array of 16 sealed beam lamps and a fog signal of eight horns with a range of five miles.

### Refreshments

There are no refreshments available on the Calf. As it is a glorious place for a picnic in good weather, be sure to bring food and drink yourself.

### Public Transport

For fares and departure times for the boat trips around and/or for landing on the Calf, telephone (01624) 832339.

*The ruins of Rushen Abbey, Ballasalla.*

# ROUTE 5                                    5.5 miles

## Silverdale

**Outline**

Rushen Abbey - Silverdale Glen - Grenaby - Ballahot - Rushen Abbey

**Summary**

Although this walk is not very long, the second leg, on leaving the Silverdale Glen, would be difficult for children under about 12 years of age. For this reason, there is an alternative route given which, though a little longer, would be no trouble to a child of about six and over. In summer, this walk is likely to be reasonably dry throughout its length, but walking boots are desirable.

**Attractions**

The ruins of Rushen Abbey lie on the left bank of the Silverburn river. The grounds also contain many graves, including those of three Viking kings of Man who died in the Island between 1235 and 1265. Rushen Abbey itself was founded in 1154. In the 13th century, the Cistercian order of monks there commenced writing the 'Chronicon Manniae', which was the earliest recorded history of the Island. (It is hoped that this historic site will be purchased by the Isle of Man government and opened to the public.)

Pedestrians can cross the river at this point by a footbridge, and cars by a ford, the road beyond leading to Ballasalla village. About three hundred yards further up-river there is the Monk's Bridge which was erected in the 13th century. Its width of four feet was just adequate for the packhorses it was intended to serve.

The lower portion of the Silverdale Glen is an enchanting wooded area, with the Silverburn River running through it. The banks are redolent of wild garlic and pocketed with bunches of primroses and violets in the spring. Further up the glen, at the site of what used to be an old water-mill, there is a restaurant, craft centre, shops, rowing and paddle boats for hire on a lake, a gnomes' grotto, swings, seesaw, slide and a water-powered roundabout. The latter can be stopped and started by pulling a lever which diverts the water running through the old mill's lead on to, or away from, the waterwheel which powers it. This is a most intriguing and ingenious mechanism which can be easily worked by children. Picnic tables and benches are scattered about the area for families spending the day there.

**Refreshments**

Ye Olde Abbey Inn and the Silverdale Glen Restaurant.

**Public Transport**

By bus: Douglas Bus Station. Service Nos 1A, 1C and 2 to Ballasalla.
By train: Douglas Steam Railway Station to Ballasalla.

# Route 5

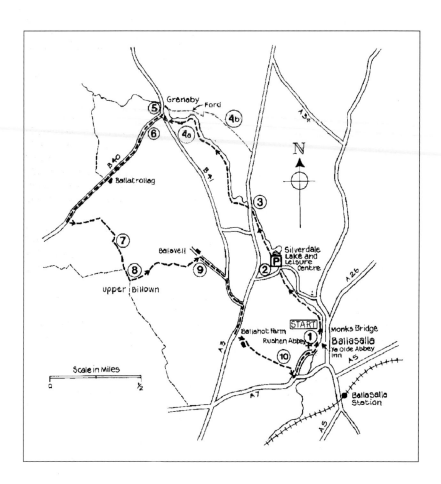

# ROUTE 5                     5.5 miles
## Silverdale

**Start**

*If the public car park in front of Ye Olde Abbey Inn - in fact a not-so-old public house next to the gates of Rushen Abbey - is full, there is plenty of space off the road to the right of or behind the public house. OS Sheet 95 (GR 278702).*

**Route**

1. *From the car park, walk up the track on the left side of the river, past the attractive little house called North Abbey, and use the stone steps at the Monk's Bridge to get into the field beyond. A track indicates the route which leads to a wooden gate giving access to the Silverdale Glen. Use any of the footpaths which lead up the glen to where it is bisected by a small metalled road.*

2. *Cross the road to the boating lake and leisure centre. Make a point of seeing the water-driven roundabout before continuing up the glen beside the river and/or mill lead.*

3. *The main glen comes to an end when it debouches on to the Castletown/Kirk Michael road. Although, like all main roads used in this book, it carries mainly private vehicles and local delivery vans - not the commercial traffic seen on main UK roads - it should be treated with care. There are now two options to this second leg of the walk: (a) directly across the road where the track continues, or (b) walking to the right on the road for about 500 yards and taking the lane on the left side by a fingerpost marked Public Footpath to Grenaby (although most of the white lettering on it seems to have come off and made it pretty illegible).*

4a. *The track mentioned as the first option, although more direct, soon becomes a tortuous footpath, which not only twists and turns through this heavily wooded area but seldom keeps on the level until it emerges from the trees. Soon after reaching a small footbridge, it becomes easier as it passes through a slightly flatter area, although this is dotted with clumps of gorse and bracken.*

    *A ladderstile leads into a field eventually and a further ladderstile gives access to a second field where a fingerpost, sitting on the banks of the river which has hitherto been largely hidden by trees, reassures the walker that he or she is on the right track. Upon reaching the fingerpost, turn directly away from the river, which begins to curl to the left into a wooded cutting. Walk up the field to the left of the woods until a wooden fence, easily crossed, appears on the right. Step over this and walk along the field high above the river until a ladderstile can be seen on the left. Cross this and turn right along the road it gives access to until you reach a Y road junction. This is a little to the left of the small collection of houses known as Grenaby and dotted around the road bridge over the Silverburn river.*

4b. *The alternative route to Grenaby is very much easier. Cross the stone stile which leads into a short length of lane. After crossing a second stile at the end of the lane, walk through the two fields ahead (separated by a kissing gate). At the edge of the farthest field, there are steps up to a third stone stile. Cross this and turn directly*

*The boating lake in Silverdale Glen.*

*The water-powered children's roundabout in Silverdale Glen.*

*left on to a track which almost immediately makes a right turn to lead you past the ruins of farm buildings (called tholtans in the Isle of Man) and down to a footbridge over a small stream. Climbing the ladderstile on the opposite bank, head for the wooden twin-legged electricity cable support and then continue walking in the same direction through a second field which runs alongside the river. A small wooden gate at the far end of that field leads on to a metalled road. Turn left, cross the road bridge over the river at Grenaby and walk up to the Y road junction mentioned above.*

5. *For the walkers who used the 4a route, turn left at the Y junction on to the road to Ballabeg. For the walkers who used the 4b route, walk straight ahead as this will get you on to the road to Ballabeg.*

6. *As you walk along this road, more and more of the Island's southern coastline will be revealed, from Langness in the east to Port St Mary in the west. After just under one mile from the junction, you will see a small green walker's sign on the left hand side of the road. Ignore it and continue until at just over a mile from the junction you will see a very much more prominent sign on the right side of the road reading Public Footpath Grenaby Road and pointing to a track on the left of the road. This looks rather like someone's drive, which in effect it is, but walk along it past a house called Lower Ballavarkish and take the footpath which is clearly marked on the right.*

7. *This leads to a rough track across three fields, with marks showing the way. The track ends at the entrance to a farmyard, but you should continue along the left hand edge of this third field until you see a small wooden gate on the left. This is not way-marked, but go through it, cross the little bridge and look out for a fingerpost beyond it.*

8. *At the foot of the fingerpost there is a ladderstile which you should cross. The wide stone track on which you will then find yourself leads to the farm on the left, so turn right. When you see another fingerpost beside a green metal kissing gate on your left, the track turns sharply to the right and soon afterwards there is a turning off to the left. Take this and follow the track as it leads past Ballavell Farm and brings you out on to a small metalled country road.*

9. *Turn right at the road and then right again as you once more meet the Castletown/Kirk Michael road. Stick to the left hand side of it, where you will soon find a pavement. After 300 yards, you will see the whitewashed gate pillars of Ballahot Farm on the left. A signpost opposite the pillars indicates that the route through the farm is a footpath to Ballasalla village. Take the wide gateway which leads out of the farmyard you will shortly encounter, and follow the lane until you see a small blue-painted gate on the left of the track with a larger blue gate on the right.*

10. *Take the smaller blue gate - it has a stone stile on its right - and walk along the grassy pathway beyond. It passes an imposing house on the right and leads to a wider track, dropping gently downhill. After taking the first left at the end of the track, you will find yourself at the rear of Rushen Abbey and Ye Olde Abbey Inn.*

*The Tynwald Ceremony*

*St John's Chapel from Tynwald Hill*

# ROUTE 6                3.5 miles
## St Johns

**Outline**

Tynwald National Park & Arboretum, St Johns - Sunny Bank - Poortown - Tynwald Hill, St Johns

**Summary**

If the weather has been wet this makes a good walk, since the mixture of tracks and metalled country lanes is unlikely to lead to wet feet. As the walk is in the centre of the Island, it is the area least likely to be assailed by strong winds. Ordinary outdoor walking shoes are adequate.

**Attractions**

Tynwald (ancient Norse, *Thing-vollr* meaning assembly field) is the Manx form of government, the oldest continuous parliamentary government in the world. Some time in the 9th century, Viking settlers in Man inaugurated their *Thing*, disdaining the existing Celtic law and customs, the two forms of government functioning independently. When the Viking Godred Crovan I invaded Man in 1079 and beat the Manx in battle, he became King of Man. He abolished the Celtic form of government altogether and confirmed the Norse system as the national government.

The Tynwald National Park & Arboretum was established in 1979 to commemorate the millennium (1,000 years) of Tynwald. Trees were donated by the governments of a large number of countries to mark the occasion and since then other trees and shrubs have been added. It is a pleasant and restful place with the gifts from foreign governments marked.

Although it is a few hundred yards off the route of this walk, the Tynwald Craft Centre is worth a visit if time permits either on the outward leg of the walk or on the return.

Tynwald Hill is an artificial four-tiered conical mound of grass-covered earth said to have been brought from the Island's 17 parishes, thereby symbolising the whole Island. Each tier is about three feet high with the top tier (about 17 ft in diameter) approached by a flight of steps cut into the turf directly facing the Royal Chapel of St John.

Normally, the Court of Tynwald's members meet throughout the year in Douglas, the capital. But the original principles of *Thing-Vollr* is still the basis of the Manx constitution. Thus, annually on Old Midsummer's Day (5th July), the King (represented by the Lt-Governor), Deemsters (High Court Judges) the elected members of the Keys (the lower House), the appointed members of the Legislative Council (the upper House) and a number of civic authorities meet to give effect to the laws by the Deemsters promulgating them in Manx and English to the electorate. Members of the electorate may present Petitions for the Redress of Grievance to

*(Continued on page 40)*

## Route 6

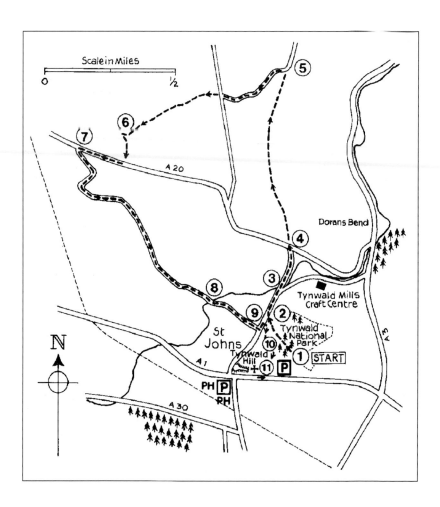

# ROUTE 6

**3.5 miles**

## St Johns

### Start

*At the free car park outside the Tynwald National Park & Arboretum. OS Sheet 95 (GR 283818).*

### Route

1. Enter the Tynwald National Park & Arboretum via the gate adjacent to the car park and study the large-scale diagram of the park there. It matters not which 'ride' you take through the park, but your ultimate destination is marked 12 on the diagram, being the north-west corner of the park.

2. Climb over the two stiles there. They give access to a small road on the left. Join it and turn right. Although the road is narrow, the slow speed traffic on it can be heavy, as it is the main means of getting to the Tynwald Mills Craft Centre. Care should therefore be exercised for the three or four hundred yards walking along this road. As the Craft Centre is on the road to the right just before the road bridge ahead, such traffic as there is will be going that way.

3. Walk over the road bridge and continue along the road, which now climbs steeply but is virtually traffic-free. It soon debouches on to a main east/west road between Glen Helen and Peel.

4. Cross the main road and take the wide farm track directly opposite, signposted Starvey. This continues to climb uphill with pleasing views of the countryside all round. Behind you the village of St Johns nestles beneath the impressive height of Slieu Whallian hill (1,092 ft).

5. At the point where the track joins a metalled country road turn left, following it to the first crossroads. Cross the north/south road and continue straight ahead up another wide farm track.

6. The track turns sharply to the left, at which point you will be able to look down on to a large quarry. Blasting occasionally takes place there, but according to a notice on the track this can only take place at 9.45, 12 noon or 2.30pm. As the track turns to the left, it begins to lose altitude until it reaches the Glen Helen/Peel road again where you turn right. This is a wide road with fast-moving traffic, so for the 450 yards along which it is necessary to use it, care should be taken to keep well into the right hand side.

7. Upon reaching the entrance gates to the Poortown Quarry, cross the road and take the small country lane on the left. This lane wanders lethargically between fields

*in a seemingly haphazard manner, but the countryside is a delight, softer and more lush than can be found in most other parts of the Island.*

8. *The lane eventually becomes a ford across a small river with a footbridge above it. Although thereafter a road comes in to join the lane from the left, carry straight on until it meets the road between your point of exit from the park and the road bridge mentioned in 3 above.*

9. *Re-enter the park at the point where you left it on the outward leg of the walk and take the first or second 'ride' leading uphill on the right.*

10. *This will soon bring you to a hedge bordering the area of the Tynwald Hill. Walk along the hedge until you arrive at a small wooden gate opposite a large mounted boulder, the Millennium Stone set there to mark Tynwald's millennium in 1979.*

11. *After passing through the gate, you can either inspect the Tynwald Hill on the right or go straight on to look at the unusual seating arrangements in the Royal Chapel of St John. The Tynwald exhibition in the hall next to the chapel can also be visited before making your way back to the car park.*

*(Continued from page 37)*

Tynwald at that time. These annual outdoor Tynwalds have at times been held at Cronk Urleigh (see Route 15) and at Cronk Keeill Abban behind St Luke's Church (see Route 10), but in modern times they have all been held at St Johns and are the most colourful event in the Island's calendar.

The Royal Chapel of St John is unusual. At the conclusion of the Tynwald Day ceremony, often presided over by members of the British royal family and occasionally by HM the Queen, whose title is Lord of Man, the Lt-Governor and members of the government retire to the chapel in which each member's seat bears his name and the business of government is there concluded. The chapel's strange seating arrangement is to facilitate this event.

An exhibition next to the chapel explains all aspects of the history and customs of Tynwald. Entrance is free.

**Refreshments**

There are two public houses and a restaurant in St Johns.

**Public Transport**

By bus: Douglas Bus Station, services No 4, 5, 5A, 6, 6A.

# ROUTE 7                                            4.5 miles
## The Marine Drive

**Outline**

Douglas/Port Soderick Halt - Port Soderick Glen & Cove - Marine Drive - Douglas Head - Douglas

**Summary**

The short steam railway journey is a novel start to this very easy walk. The main part of it is on the Marine Drive, which runs along the edge of spectacular cliffs on the east coast. Thanks to a cliff fall some 10 years ago which took a part of the road with it, the road is no longer open to through traffic. Such cars that go along the short stretches of it at either end of the drive are mainly owned by walkers wishing to exercise themselves and/or their dogs.

There is a pavement, largely neglected through lack of use, along the entire length of the walk. Ordinary walking shoes are all that are necessary.

**Attractions**

The short journey by the Victorian steam train will be enjoyed by the children at least. Port Soderick Glen and cove are attractive spots. The walk, once you are on the Marine Drive, is almost completely flat and the road is metalled.

Below Douglas Head, there is the lighthouse overlooking the wide entrance to Douglas harbour, built in 1832. Above it but below and not visible from Douglas Head road (which meets the Douglas end of the Marine Drive) is the Camera Obscura, under restoration in 1997. Built in about 1880, it has eleven viewing turrets and gives panoramic views of Douglas. It is basically a darkened room in which periscopes reflecting light through lenses throw images of different sectors of Douglas on to white matt surfaces. The only other known survivor of this type of Victorian entertainment is in Edinburgh.

The Tower of Refuge, a notable landmark in Douglas Bay, sits on the Conister rocks, just beyond the outer harbour breakwaters. The refuge for wrecked sailors was built in 1833 as a result of the spectacular destruction of a paddle steamer called the *St George* two years earlier on those rocks as well as many other vessels before her. The prime mover of the tower's erection was Sir William Hillary who, at 59 years of age, helmed one of the lifeboats which took part in the rescue of all the crew. He had founded the National Lifeboat Institution in 1824 and this subsequently came to be called the Royal National Lifeboat Institution. His remains lie in St George's churchyard in Douglas.

*HMS Ranger,* a warship engaged in hunting for smugglers in the Irish Sea in the
*(Continued on page 45)*

# Route 7

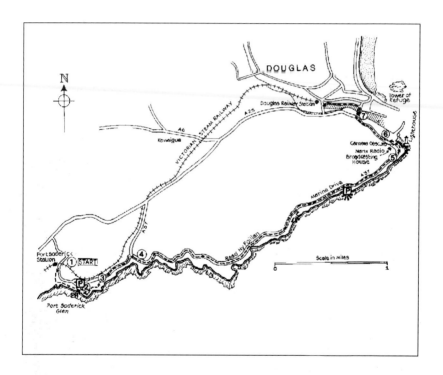

# ROUTE 7 4.5 miles
## The Marine Drive

**Start**

*At the car park in Douglas Steam Railway Station. OS Sheet 95 (GR 378753).*

**Route**

*1. Take the train to Port Soderick Halt, the first stop on the line. Upon leaving the station, turn right along the small road which passes under the railway lines. Take the first entrance to the right which leads into Port Soderick Glen, and then follow the first footpath off to the left, walking down the wide grassy sward of the glen until you arrive at Port Soderick cove.*

*2. Turn left and walk in front of the public house, taking the footpath which turns inland just before a stone archway. (The footpath which goes under the archway and along the rocks comes to a dead end).*

*3. Climb the long flights of steps which ascend the cliffs above Port Soderick and walk along the grassy lane until you join a metalled road.*

*4. The road swings a little inland before straightening out to join the Marine Drive along the top of the cliffs. After a few minutes' walk you will pass through a kissing*

*Douglas Harbour with the Tower of Refuge on the extreme right.*

*The Douglas end of Marine Drive.*

*gate which blocks off all road traffic until you have walked almost the entire length of the Drive. You will know the end of the Drive is near when you pass under a large stone double archway.*

5. *Just as you reach the first building on the Douglas Head road, which joins up with the Marine Drive, take the footpath to the right between some green-painted metal uprights. This leads downhill towards the Douglas Head lighthouse and then, as it curves to the left, there are good views of the Tower of Refuge, the Camera Obscura and Douglas harbour.*

6. *The footpath joins up with the Douglas Head road. Walk down the pavement on this road past a number of houses until you reach an opening on the right hand side leading to a wide flight of steps.*

7. *The steps lead down to a lower road running along the South Quay of the harbour. Directly opposite the foot of the flight of steps is a metal footbridge which usually enables pedestrians to cross the harbour to North Quay. It is, however, a swing bridge and if it is closed to pedestrians it is to enable vessels to leave or enter harbour. In that case, turn left along South Quay and take the first right at the inland end of the harbour. Upon leaving the footbridge, turn left and walk along the North Quay to the far end of the harbour where Douglas Steam Railway Station is located.*

*(Continued from page 41)*

1770s, was based in Douglas, to which it had often to return for repairs. On board was 20 year old Cornish midshipman William Bligh, and it was during his time on board the *Ranger* that he met Betsy Betham, whom he married in 1781. He was also to meet here the high-born Manxmen Fletcher Christian and Peter Heywood, both of whom subsequently sailed in *HMS Bounty* on its ill-fated voyage to Tahiti.

**Refreshments**

There is a public house facing the cove of Port Soderick.

**Public Transport**

By bus: Douglas Bus Station. Service No 29 Monday-Saturday.

By train: Douglas Steam Railway Station. Trains run from April to end September, seven days a week.

## Route 8

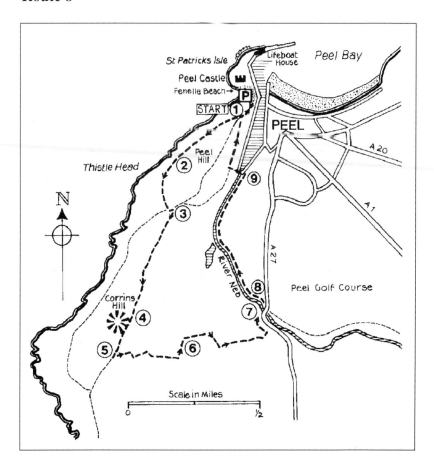

# ROUTE 8                                          3 miles
## Peel

**Outline**

St Patrick's Isle, Peel - Peel Head - The Raggatt - Peel Harbour - St Patrick's Isle

**Summary**

This short walk gives good views of the spectacular western coastline down as far as the Calf of Man as well as of Peel town, harbour and castle. After a rugged start walking up to the summit of Peel Head, there is a pleasantly sheltered conclusion strolling along the quietly flowing River Neb. Outdoor walking shoes will suffice, but walking boots are preferable.

**Attractions**

The main point of interest is Peel Castle, which stands on St Patrick's Isle. The isle is connected to the Island by a short causeway. The castle's imposing curtain wall encircles the ruins of St Patrick's Church and the Round Tower from the 11th century, the 13th century Cathedral of St German and the later apartments of the Lords of Man. In the 11th century, the castle became the ruling seat of the Norse Kingdom of Man and the Isles. Recent archaeological excavation unearthed the Norse period grave of a high-born lady whose buried jewellery and effects can now be seen in the Manx Museum. There is an entrance fee, the entrance being a short distance from the car park at the start of this walk.

On the town side of the harbour is the Manx National Heritage Centre. Modern display techniques illustrate its three main themes: the early Celtic inhabitants and their lifestyle, the Vikings' political and cultural influence on the Island and Man's maritime tradition. Incorporated in the Centre is *Odin's Raven,* a replica of the famous Gokstad Ship excavated from a Viking burial site near Oslo. The replica was built in, and sailed over from, Norway in 1979.

Corrin's Folly on Peel Head is alleged to have been intended as a mausoleum built by one Corrin who was a staunch Non-Conformist and objected to being buried on consecrated ground. However, on his death his family had him buried in the churchyard notwithstanding his past convictions. The tower is about 50 ft high on four floors with an internal flight of steps and contains 12 memorial tablets. The low-walled burial ground in front of it is said to contain the remains of his wife and child, who predeceased him.

**Refreshments**

There are a number of public houses, restaurants and shops of all kinds in Peel itself. There are public toilets just beyond Peel Castle entrance, between the RNLI lifeboat station and the long harbour breakwater.

**Public transport**

By bus: Douglas Bus Station. Service Nos 4, 4A, 5, 5A, 6, 6A.

# ROUTE 8                  3 miles
## Peel

### Start

*At the free car park just before the causeway to St Patrick's Isle (OS Sheet 95, GR 243845), facing Fenella Beach on the left side of the causeway.*

### Route

*1. Take the steps and concrete pathway on the inland side of the car park and, on reaching a wider concrete track, turn right towards the cliffs bordering the sea.*

*2. The track is wide until it reaches the chute (which you might smell before you get there) by which lorries carrying the discarded shells of the Manx shellfish known as Queenies dispose of them down the cliff side. There are railings and a gate on the cliff edge at this point. Carry on past the railings up a steeply climbing footpath which leads inland through a green-painted kissing gate.*

*3. Eschew the temptation of turning to the right when your footpath, which continues to climb inexorably upwards, crosses a wide level track leading seawards.*

*4. After breasting two hills and leaving a pair of posts carrying an array of radio aerials on your left, you will see the square tower of Corrin's Folly ahead, with its satellite obelisks located around it on Peel Head. A little to the left of the Folly as you pass it is a 'trig point'. Just in front of the tower is a low-walled burial patch.*

*5. The path now descends to the corner where two stone walls converge. At this point turn left, keeping the stone wall which drops downhill on your right through a bracken-covered field.*

*6. At the bottom of the field, you will see a ladderstile on the right. Climb over it and turn left into a short length of road with a farmhouse on the right. Take the first left and follow the lane as it makes two right turns and a left turn before dropping more steeply downhill with a zigzag in it to where it debouches on to a metalled road at an area known as The Raggatt.*

*7. Cross the road with care and walk over the road bridge, keeping to the right hand side of it. The bridge crosses the River Neb, and as you cross it you will see an opening in the right hand retaining wall which gives access to a flight of wooden steps leading down to the river.*

8. *Find your way to the wide track running parallel to the river, opposite an old mill building. Turn left and follow the track past the power station to the inland end of the harbour.*

9. *Turn left over the road bridge here and on reaching the opposite side walk up the short flight of steps ahead to a footpath which runs parallel to the road running alongside the harbour. This footpath ends when it joins the short concrete footpath and steps leading to the Fenella Beach car park.*

*Peel Castle on St. Patrick's Isle.*

*Cass ny Hawin Gorge, Santon.*

# ROUTE 9                    7 miles
## Derbyhaven

**Outline**

Ballasalla - Castletown - Derbyhaven - Cass ny Hawin Gorge - Balthane - Ballasalla

**Summary**

Although this is a long walk, it is almost totally on the flat and very easy going. A footpath by the Silverburn River leads to Castletown harbour, and from there to Derbyhaven the route is on quiet little roads. The road comes to an end after Derbyhaven and thenceforth the way is on footpaths to Cass ny Hawin Gorge and on a little-used road to Balthane. Ballasalla itself is on a main road, but after about 400 yards the walk ends on another small road. Ordinary outdoor walking shoes will suffice.

**Attractions**

The walk begins near Rushen Abbey whose history is described in Route 5, and Castletown's Castle Rushen and the Nautical Museum are described in Route 3.

Between Castletown and Derbyhaven the buildings and grounds of King William's College, a co-educational public school, can be seen on the left of the road. This was built in 1833, was wholly destroyed by fire in 1844 and rebuilt in 1863. It has since been extended and modernised at various times. Between it and the seashore is the ruin incorrectly called Hango Hill, a place of execution in days gone by. In fact its correct name is Mount Strange, the ruin being that of a summer house! Hango Hill is located somewhere under the College's playing fields.

Ronaldsway Airport's perimeter touches the College boundaries on their northern and eastern sides, and traffic lights on the road just past the College are to halt traffic while planes are landing or taking off on the short and not often used runway. Just past the traffic lights, the 10th green of the Castletown Golf Links (one of eight golf courses on the Island) can be seen. This is the area of the peninsula known as Langness where the first Derby horse race took place. It was inaugurated by James, the seventh Earl of Derby and Lord of Man, in 1627. It was not transferred to England until 1779.

Derbyhaven is a small bay popular with sailors and water-skiers. Around it is a collection of houses and the Castletown Golf Links Hotel. Originally established in 1507 by the Earls of Derby (members of the family were Lords of Man between 1460 and 1736), it was the Island's chief fishing port in the 17th century. It was earlier called *Rognvalds-vagr* (Norse for Reginald's or Ronald's Bay after the Scandinavian king who landed there in 1226). It had a tumultuous history, being used by a number of attackers of the Island, including Robert Bruce who landed there in 1313 to lay seige to Castle Rushen.

Ronaldsway Airport now covers the site of the Battle of Ronaldsway in 1270, but a plaque on the side of the road leading around towards the Manx Flyers' Club at the north-east side of Derbyhaven marks the spot. *(Continued on page 54)*

## Route 9

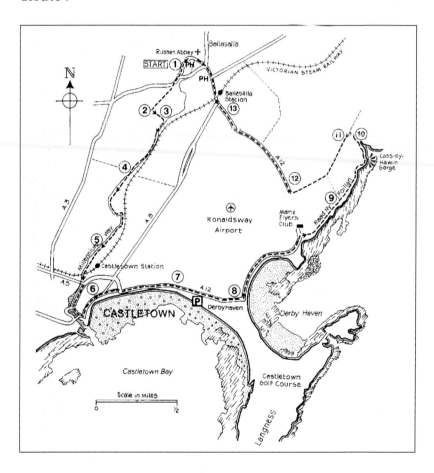

# ROUTE 9
## Derbyhaven

**7 miles**

### Start

*At the off-road free car parking area to the right of Ye Olde Abbey Inn, which is beside Rushen Abbey. (See start of Route 5).*

### Route

1. *Take the small road passing behind the Inn. Cross over the Ballasalla/Ballabeg road it joins, walk a few dozen paces to the right and you will see a wide track, the entrance to which is marked by the stylised three-legs sign denoting the Millennium Way.*

2. *The track comes to an end as it enters a farmyard, but turn left down a grassy lane in front of the yard and follow it through a metal kissing gate and between some derelict farm buildings until the Silverburn River appears directly ahead.*

3. *Turn right and follow the path with the river on your left and the steam railway lines on the opposite bank. The strange white railings to be seen in the middle of a field on the right are the remains of a horse racing course no longer in use.*

4. *At the wooden footbridge over the river, cross to the opposite bank and continue following the path which keeps roughly parallel to the river as it twists and turns.*

5. *The path becomes narrower as it passes between the river and a sports playing ground (Poulsom Park) where there is also a children's playground equipped with swings, slide, etc. Soon after walking under a railway bridge, the path debouches on to the main Castletown/Port St Mary road.*

6. *Cross over this road and continue walking downstream as the river widens into the upper part of Castletown harbour. The road soon forks, one going over a road bridge into Castletown itself and the other turning left alongside the harbour and past the Nautical Museum. Take the latter, which makes a sharp turn to the left just after the Nautical Museum and runs parallel to the seashore.*

7. *Keep to the succession of small roads which stick closely to the seashore. King William's College and the Ronaldsway Airport runways appear on the left, and Castletown Golf Links on the right.*

8. *Upon entering Derbyhaven village, turn left by the shore and continue around the perimeter of the airport. The road ends as it enters the Manx Flyers' Club grounds, but a footpath continues along the shore line, passing under the yellow metal gantry which stretches out into the sea and holds the airport's main runway approach lights.*

9. *A walking sign pointing to the left soon afterwards can be used as a shorter way back to Ballasalla, but to use it would mean missing the rather spectacular Cass ny Hawin Gorge a quarter of a mile further along the coast.*

10. *Turn left at the gorge and follow it upstream until the path swings away to the right. You will see there is a gap in the stone wall straight ahead at this point. Walk through the gap, turn left and follow the grassy lane until it stops before a stile.*

11. *Go over the stile and turn left again along a wide track which eventually turns sharp right and becomes a metalled road, running along the north side of the airport perimeter.*

12. *Continue straight ahead on this road as it passes through Balthane's small industrial estate by the airport and joins the main Ballasalla/Castletown road.*

13. *Turn right at the main road and follow it over the steam railway level crossing to the little road roundabout. Continue straight on, with the Whitestone Inn on your left, reaching a second small roundabout in about two hundred yards. Directly ahead you will see the road called Mill Road, and this will lead you to the footbridge by a ford over the Silverburn River. On the opposite bank is your car parking area.*

*(Continued from page 51)*

Cass ny Hawin Gorge is situated at the mouth of the Santon Burn and Glen. It is a spectacular ravine guarded at one time by a Celtic hill fort overbuilt with a Viking house.

**Refreshments**

There are several food and confectionery shops, public houses and restaurants in Ballasalla and Castletown. Both places have public toilets.

**Public transport**

By bus: Douglas Bus Station to Ballasalla. Service Nos 1, 1A, 1C, 2, 2A.
By train: Douglas Steam Railway Station to Ballasalla Station.

# ROUTE 10                                        7 miles

## Baldwin Valley

### Outline

Injebreck House - Brandywell Road - Millennium Way - St Luke's Church - West Baldwin Reservoir - Injebreck House

### Summary

This walk, both in length and terrain, is the most challenging and the only one in the book which climbs up to a part of the fells. At two points it ascends above the 1,500 ft contour. The track is inclined to be rough in places and, although outdoor walking shoes will suffice, boots would be preferable.

### Attractions

Injebreck (Old Norse; 'End slope') House and estate lies on the end slope which seals the northern end of the Baldwin Valley. Below it is the West Baldwin reservoir which looks like a natural lake and greatly enhances the outstanding beauty of this area. The construction of the reservoir was started in 1900 and by the time it had filled in 1905 it had submerged three farms and two cottages. It serves the needs of the capital Douglas and its surrounding districts, having a capacity of 301 million gallons, a depth of over 70 feet when full and a length of 3/4 mile.

Injebreck House was once a hotel with lovely gardens, a huge pavilion with bars, and the largest dance floor of any seaside watering place. A great favourite weekend haunt for the gentry of Douglas, they used to come out in hundreds, being transported by landaus or charabancs. It is now privately owned.

For the walker, the main attractions of this walk are the open hill country to which it ascends, the superb views of large parts of the northern half of the Island - including Snaefell mountain (2,036 ft) - the ever-curious hares which abound, the birds of prey quartering the ground in search of a meal, and the skylarks whose tuneful song is constantly heard overhead though the birds themselves remain strangely invisible.

### Refreshments

There are no refreshments available here.

### Public transport

There is no access by public transport to this area.

## Route 10

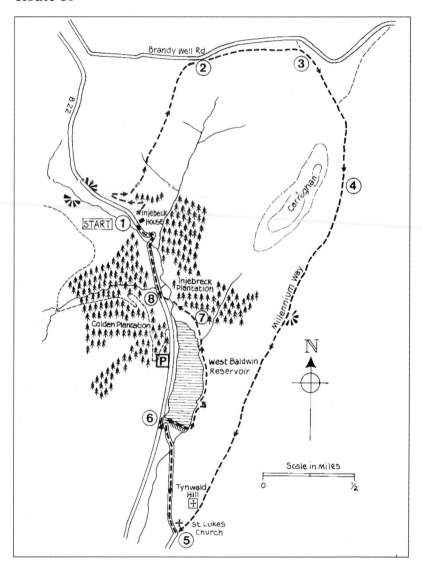

# ROUTE 10                                    7 miles
## Baldwin Valley

### Start

*To reach Injebreck House, take the A1 westward from Douglas, joining the A23 at Braddan Bridge. After 2 miles turn right at Mount Rule, at which point there is a signpost indicating West Baldwin. Continue straight on through Baldwin village, after which the reservoir appears on your right. After passing the reservoir, the road makes a sharp uphill turn to the left and Injebreck House is the only building on the right. Just uphill from Injebreck House, there is a yellow-painted cattle grid and beyond it a small 'green' beside the road with a solitary tree on it. Cars can be parked beside the 'green' off the road. OS Sheet 95 (GR 355848).*

### Route

*1. A track adjacent to the car parking area leads gently uphill towards a plantation of conifers. Just before reaching the plantation, the track turns left and thereafter zigzags upwards between fields, passing through a farm gate and a box wire openable fence.*

*2. At the end of the track there is a farm gate which gives access to the Brandywell Road. However, do not go through it, but instead turn right and walk parallel to the wire fencing running beside the road.*

*You will now be at 1,300 ft with the fields giving way to heather and the two masts at the summit of Snaefell in sight ahead.*

*3. After passing a green mound on the left, join a well-defined, stony track coming in from the road to take you gently uphill to the right. You will soon see and join up with the Millennium Way, a walk which starts at Sky Hill in the north of the Island and ends at Castletown in the south. It is distinguished by a waymark which is a stylised form of three legs within a circle.*

*At this point the 1,500 ft contour is reached and thereafter it's downhill all the way. After passing through a farm gate, continue along the straight, stony track ahead.*

*4. On the left there is the deep valley of East Baldwin, on the right is the 1,600 ft hill called Caraghan. After passing through two metal gates, the track becomes low enough in altitude to regain grass fields on either side. Two further metal gates later, you will pass a plantation on the right and shortly afterwards catch sight of St Luke's Church ahead.*

*When you see it, keep an eye open for a stone stile on the right hand side of the track. If you climb over it and walk a few yards to your right, there is a stone circular constructon with a notice reading 'Site of Tynwald, holden at Killabane 1428'. (The explanation of Tynwald is given in Route 6).*

5. *St Luke's Church lies on the corner of a small country road, so turn right there and continue the descent until, after passing over a stone bridge, the road curves upwards and joins a wider road running along the left (or west) side of the reservoir.*

6. *Turn right on to this road and then right again through some green-painted metal gates giving access to the top of the grassy dam which contains the reservoir's water. Carry on to the far side of the dam, pass through a small wooden gate and turn left along a narrow path which leads up the right side of the dam and is used mainly by keen trout fishermen. There are rather a lot of gorse bushes pressing close to the footpath initially, but they should not prove too difficult to avoid. At all times, stick to the footpath closest to the water.*

7. *As you reach the far end of the reservoir, climb over a low stile and through a gap in the bank ahead. Turn half left and continue walking away from the reservoir until in 200 yards you come across a wide stone track. Turn left on to this and follow it over a small bridge and on to the road which skirted the left (west) side of the reservoir.*

8. *Turn right on to this and follow it uphill past Injebreck House and back to the car parking spot.*

*Injebreck Reservoir in the Baldwin Valley*

# ROUTE 11
3 miles
## The Laxey Wheel

**Outline**

Laxey Harbour - Laxey Glen Gardens - 'Lady Isabella' waterwheel and Mines Trail - Laxey Valley Gardens - St George's Woollen Mills - Laxey Harbour

**Summary**

Starting at the harbour side in Old Laxey, the walk is by a footpath up Laxey Glen beside the river to the Glen Gardens, passing on the way the Laxey Flour Mills and Laxey Electric Railway Station. It then continues to the unique 'Lady Isabella' waterwheel and Mines Trail, through the Laxey Valley Gardens to St George's Woollen Mills and then back, on the opposite side of the river, to the harbour.

**Attractions**

Laxey is derived from the Scandinavian word *Iara*, meaning salmon river.

Old Laxey Harbour is the prettiest of all the Island's harbours, very like some of the small Cornish harbours. The tall stone building beside it manufactures briar and meerschaum tobacco smoking pipes. Meerschaum comes from Somalia and is a hard white chalk-like substance which is ideal for making cool smoking pipes. The Laxey factory is the only one in the world making meerschaum pipes in quantity. Pipes can be bought from a shop on the premises.

Laxey beach is a mixture of shingle and sand, and at either end of the promenade there are toilets. Laxey Glen Gardens are in New Laxey (further inland and higher up the glen). They make a pleasant stop for a rest and have a children's playground, paddling pool, ballroom, restaurant and toilets.

Laxey Electric Railway Station is unusual and rather pretty. It has no platforms, but, apart from being the halfway stop on the Douglas/Ramsey route, it is also the terminus for the Manx Mountain Railway which runs up to the summit of Snaefell (2,036 ft). This is a not-to-be-missed excursion for a clear sunny day.

At a point where the Mountain Railway lines cross the main road, there is a blacksmith's yard which displays a most intriguing collection of ancient farm machinery. The walk continues up Mines Road opposite the Laxey Heritage Trust Information Centre and Gift Shop. To really appreciate the ingenuity and historic origins of the unique 'Lady Isabella' waterwheel - almost certainly the largest working waterwheel in the world - it is very desirable to pick up some literature about it and the Mines Trail which surrounds it. It is a truly remarkable example of a beautifully restored piece of industrial archaeology.

The wheel was built in 1854 to pump water out of the mines nearby. It was named in honour of the then Lieutenant-Governor's wife. It has a diameter of 72 ft and a width of 6 ft. There are 168 buckets each holding 24 gallons of water and, until

*(Continued on page 62)*

# Route 11

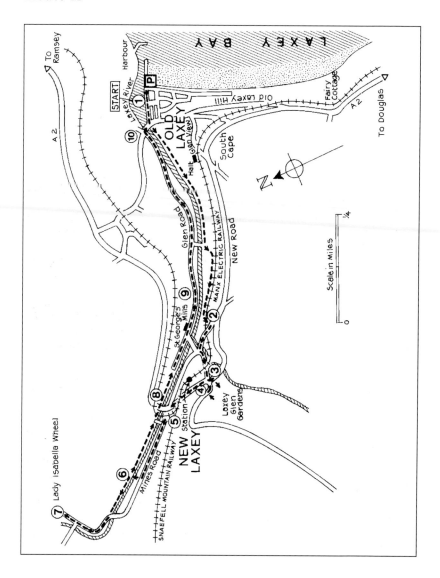

# ROUTE 11
## The Laxey Wheel
**3 miles**

### Start

*Laxey is 8 miles along the A2 road from Douglas. Branch right down Old Laxey Hill at Fairy Cottage, turn right at the bottom of the hill. Free parking on harbour side and along the promenade. OS Sheet 95 (GR 444837).*

### Route

1. *From Old Laxey harbour, opposite Laxey Pipes factory, pass Laxey Yacht Club on the left and take the public footpath to the right of the Shore Hotel along the river bank. After passing a large stone building on the left, the footpath turns left and then right before running parallel to the electric railway lines (no possibility of electrocution).*

2. *Cross over the lines and take the exit marked, turning right downhill on the road. The first turning to the left is the Laxey Flour Mill, but take the second left uphill under the railway bridge.*

3. *Upon reaching the main road, turn left and cross the road opposite the Laxey Glen Hotel. The road on the left of the hotel leads to Laxey Glen Gardens and restaurant.*

4. *Retrace your steps to the main road and turn left. Laxey Station is now on the right. The blacksmith's yard is just before the Snaefell Mountain Railway lines cross the road.*

5. *After crossing the railway lines, turn left up Mines Road to the Laxey Heritage Trust Information Centre and Gift Shop, taking the footpath sloping down to the river just beyond it. Leave the toilets on your left and take the footbridge.*

6. *Turn left and walk along the footpath until a kissing gate is reached. Go through it, turn right up the lane.*

7. *The entrance to the 'Lady Isabella' waterwheel and Mines Trail is on the left. (There is a turnstile here as a small charge is made for entrance. A map of the complex mine workings is on the roadway leading to the right of the wheel).*

   *Return to the kissing gate and take the same footpath to the bridge, but continue straight on along the river bank until the footpath ends with some steps leading up to the main road again.*

8. *Cross the road and enter the Laxey Valley Gardens (toilets on the left), walking right through them and keeping close to the river until you reach St George's Woollen Mills.*

9. *Carry on down the road which leads towards Old Laxey harbour, passing numerous cottages, once the homes of miners but now being largely modernised.*

10. *At the road bridge, turn right and then left along Tent Road, which leads to the harbour.*

*(Continued from page 59)*
the mines closed in 1929, it was capable of raising 250 gallons of water per minute from 1,500 ft underground. This required power equivalent to 185 hp with the wheel at 2.5 revolutions per minute. The ingenious way in which this power was transmitted to the underground pump by means of the rod which still can be seen travelling backwards and forwards along a viaduct, and the way in which the whole mining complex was powered by streams flowing off the fells above it, is quite remarkable.

The Laxey Valley Gardens were converted from the original mines' washing floors. The lead ore was brought to the washing floors by two small steam engines, where it was crushed, cleaned and bagged before being taken in horse-drawn trucks to the beach for shipment. Laxey Fair is held in the gardens every summer.

St George's Woollen Mills, built in 1850 as corn mills, became woollen mills when rented by a skilled silk weaver named Rydings, who had come to the Island in the 1870s and who was a devoted follower of John Ruskin. He was also a Companion of Ruskin's St George's Guilds, whose main tenet was that no mechanical means should be employed in the production of goods where skilled hands could be used instead.

Rydings, seeing the harsh conditions under which women worked on the mines' washing floors, and fearing that their traditional skills of hand spinning and weaving would be lost because of their exhausting work, enlisted Ruskin's Guilds. This supplied one-third of the £500 capital needed to take over the corn mills and equip them for spinning wool from local farmers and weaving it into cloth. The gesture was rewarded by naming the mills after the Guilds. They have been operating ever since and have customers all over the world.

**Refreshments**
At the far end of Old Laxey Promenade; several restaurants and public houses in New Laxey; in Laxey Glen Gardens; near Old Laxey road bridge, Shore Hotel.

**Public transport**
By bus: Douglas Bus Station. Service No 15 to South Cape, walk downhill via Glen View road to harbour.
By electric train: Queens Promenade, Douglas Tramway terminus to South Cape, walk downhill via Glen View to harbour.

*Laxey Harbour*

# ROUTE 12              4.5 miles
## Ballaglass

**Outline**

Port Cornaa - Ballaglass Glen - Cashtal yn Ard - Glen Mona - Port Cornaa

**Summary**

This walk goes through the beautiful Ballaglass Glen, climbs up to the gaunt site of the pre-historic burial chambers of Cashtal yn Ard and then drops down again along Glen Mona to the sea at Port Cornaa. Walking boots should be worn.

**Attractions**

Port Cornaa belies its name; it isn't a port by any stretch of the imagination, but a small cove with a steep shingle beach. Inland from the beach a large lagoon is fed by two mountain streams which come together and find their outlet to the sea on the north side of the beach.

Cornaa is a Manx name and pronounced Corn-nay. It means corn water to indicate that there have been corn mills on the Cornaa streams from time immemorial.

A small hut at the southern end of the beach is where the first telegraph cable from the British mainland came ashore.

Ballaglass (*Balla*=farm, *glass*=green) Glen is a truly entrancing valley with the river which runs through it leaping over large rocks in a series of boiling falls.

The Isle of Man government's trout hatchery lies in Ballaglass Glen. Visitors are welcome to feed the fish during normal business hours.

Cashtal yn Ard (Castle of the Height) is a megalithic monument which has puzzled antiquaries of past ages, mainly because it must very early on have been opened and despoiled. It is however established as being a fine example of a 'gallery-grave' or tribal burial place. It is about 40 yards long by 15 yards wide and consists of five chambers. At the western end there is a forecourt or approach with eight large stones arranged in a semi-circle of about 12 yards in diameter.

Glen Mona stretches down to the sea at Port Cornaa and marks the northern edge of the estate known as the Barony. All the land to the right of the road leading down the glen is a part of the Barony, which was the name given to lands belonging to a religious body in years past.

**Refreshments**

There are no facilities where refreshments can be obtained.

**Public transport**

There is no public transport to Port Cornaa. It is however feasible to take an electric train from Douglas Tramway Station on Queens Promenade, Douglas to Ballaglass Halt, starting and ending the circular walk there.

## Route 12

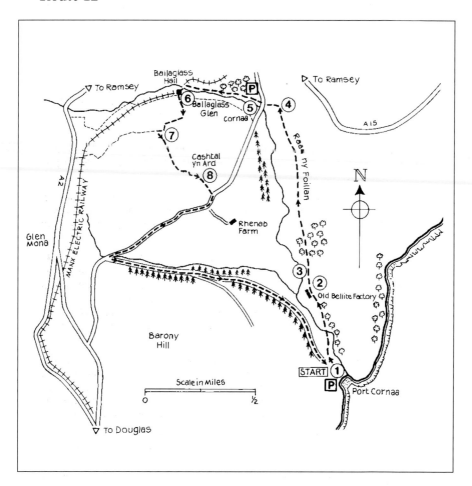

# ROUTE 12                    4.5 miles
## Ballaglass

**Start**

*At Port Cornaa, OS Sheet 95 (GR 473878). Cars can be parked at the top of the beach. From Douglas take the A2 to Ramsey via Laxey. After passing the entrance to Dhoon Glen take the first right over railway tracks and the next two successive turns to the right.*

**Route**

1. *From the top of the beach, follow a track running parallel to, and to the right of, the road to start with, but swing right when you reach the small holiday cottage and walk over the white-painted bridge beyond it. Continue along the track between fields on the left and steep sloping woodland on the right.*

2. *You will pass a strange concrete ruin of a building on the left. (Hard though it is to believe in such a sylvan setting, this was built during the First World War as a factory for making a high explosive called Bellite! The war ended before production could be started).*

3. *Pass through a tubular metal gate and swing uphill to the right, following a well-defined track. As you begin the ascent, it is worth making a short detour down to the stream on the left. There is a beautiful pool there which is refreshing on a hot day.*

4. *Continue along the track, which passes through a fine beech wood, and then take the marked cart track to the left. This leads steeply downhill to Ballaglass Glen. Before crossing the road which runs at right angles to the end of the cart track, a walk to the left up the road for about 100 yards leads to the entrance of the Isle of Man government trout hatchery, which is worth visiting if time permits. Otherwise continue the walk by going through the black iron gate marked 'Public Footpath to Ballaglass Glen' opposite the exit from the cart track.*

5. *Almost immediately after passing through the iron gate, there is a fingerpost pointing to the right marked 'Public Footpath to Cardle Veg'. Ignore this and take the smaller path ahead and a little to the left which runs along the river bank. Cross to the opposite bank by either one of the two footbridges and continue to the head of the glen where steps lead to the electric train Ballaglass Glen Halt.*

6. *Before coming abreast of the little hut at the Halt, turn left up some steps which lead behind the hut and to a decrepit iron gate at the entrance to a stony lane ahead. Follow the lane uphill and to the right. After it makes a short turn to the left and then right, a small wood appears on the left. At the far side of the wood, turn off to the left down a small track.*

7. *After passing some stone farm buildings, go through the gate which marks the end*

*of the track and walk diagonally to the left across the field to which it gives access. The Cashtal yn Ard burial ground will be quickly recognised.*

8. *Walk down the track beyond the burial site until a road is reached. Turn right and follow it as it drops gently downhill to where it crosses a ford. Just before the ford itself, take the small footbridge on the left and walk down the road through the trees of the Barony until you return to Port Cornaa.*

**Ballaglass Glen**

# ROUTE 13                     3.5 miles
# Maughold

**Outline**

Maughold Church - Port Mooar - Manx National Trust Coastal Walk - Port e Vullen - Maughold Church

**Summary**

This is a mainly coastal walk in an area of great natural beauty. Subject to the state of the tide, it can be extended from Port e Vullen to Port Lewaigue. Walking boots are desirable.

**Attractions**

The littoral scenery is in itself the main attraction of this part of the Island, but Maughold church is of historical interest. It dates from the 11th century and contains much ancient stonework. In the churchyard there is a large collection of carved stone cross-slabs of the Celtic (7th to 9th century) and Norse (10th to 11th century) periods. Among them can be seen examples of the Scandinavian ring-chain design and a beautifully engraved illustration of a typical Viking longboat.

A mile after the start of the walk there is a fine view of the Maughold Head lighthouse. It has recently been converted to automatic operation and the light keepers' premises adjacent to it have been sold to a private buyer.

In the area owned by the Manx National Trust, Manx Loghtan sheep can usually be seen. They have brown fleeces and four horns; the breed is still one of the rarest in the British Isles.

About halfway along the path through the National Trust property, a stone map-table with the surrounding area engraved on it identifies all that can be seen from that viewpoint. This includes stretches of the Scottish and English coasts from the Solway Firth, down past Sellafield to Morecambe Bay.

**Refreshments**

None available on this walk. Bring your own.

**Public transport**

By bus: Douglas Bus Station to Ramsey; service No 15. Then Ramsey to Maughold; service No 16.

By electric train: Tramway Terminus, Queens Promenade, Douglas to Ballajora Station. Alight here and take the small road leading downhill for half a mile. On the right you will then see the road marked with the sign of the white seagull on a blue background leading to Port Mooar (see part 1 of Route). Start and end your walk at Ballajora station.

# Route 13

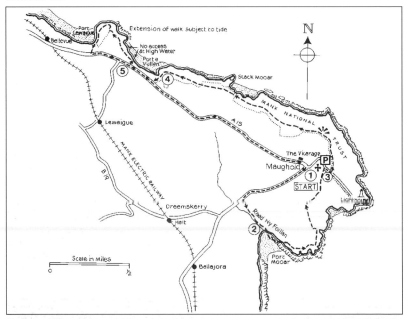

*Cashtal yn Ard*

# ROUTE 13         3.5 miles
## Maughold

### Start

*Maughold village lies about 3.5 miles south of Ramsey. From Ramsey, take the A2 road leading south towards Laxey. A mile after leaving Ramsey, branch off on to the A15. There is space to park cars outside the Old Vicarage and around the small triangular green near the gates to the churchyard. OS Sheet 95 (GR 494915).*

### Route

1. *Take the country road south-west from the car park, signposted Port Mooar. Turn first left after half a mile, down the lane marked with a sign of a white seagull on a blue background. This indicates the Raad ny Foillan (Road of the Gull), a round-the-Island coastal route of 90 miles.*

2. *At the beach, turn left and down towards the rocks at the end of the beach. A sign indicates the path which leads around Port Mooar Point. Follow the coastal footpath past a pair of fishermen's store huts, after which it turns uphill and inland. After climbing over the ladderstile, turn left along the edge of a field and then into the lane ahead. This comes out at the opposite side of the churchyard at which the car park is situated. The walk can be prematurely ended here if necessary.*

*Celtic and Norse Stone Cross Slabs, Maughold Churchyard*

*Maughold Head*

*3. Upon reaching the rear entrance to the churchyard, turn right up a small road which was primarily made to obtain access to the lighthouse. However, there is a Manx National Trust sign 100 yards up it on the left. Turn left there and walk up the track and through the nearest green kissing gate beyond. The path leads through rough grassland, home to a flock of Loghtan sheep, with fine views out to sea and, weather permitting, glimpses of England and Scotland.*

*4. The path eventually makes a left turn and leads past the gardens of two houses back to the road. As you make the left turn you will be able to look down on Port e Vullen beach and note the state of the tide. To return to Maughold, turn left upon reaching the road.*

*5. If the tide is not too high and you wish to extend the walk, turn right at the road and take the first right again, down a slipway between houses. This leads to the shingle beach. Turn left and walk along the beach until it joins a footpath leading around Gob ny Rona point to Port Lewaigue. Upon regaining the road here, turn left for Maughold.*

# ROUTE 14                  2 miles
## Sulby

### Outline

Tholt e Will Bridge - Sulby Plantation - Sulby Reservoir - Tholt e Will Glen - Tholt e Will Bridge

### Summary

This short walk from Tholt e Will Bridge is through woodland by a track leading up the Sulby River to Sulby Reservoir. After crossing the dam, a road leads into the very beautiful Tholt e Will Glen. There, paths drop through the glen down to the start of the walk. Walking boots are desirable.

### Attractions

The Sulby Glen is one of the most beautiful in the Island, and its upper part, known as Tholt e Will Glen, provides the walker with wonderfully dramatic scenery. There is a good free car park near the road bridge. Adjacent is a Celtic Crafts shop and a country style inn with tables and chairs to sit outside in good weather.

The reservoir was started in 1979 and the top water level on the dam was reached in 1983 when it was opened by HRH Princess Alexandra and the Honourable Angus Ogilvy. It has a capacity of 1,000 million gallons and a part of the drawn-off water supplies a hydro-electric generating station further down the valley.

The strange bell mouth structure emerging from the water of the reservoir is the overflow, which can draw off 4,000 gallons of water per second in case of serious flood water flowing into the reservoir. On the 'inland' side of the dam can be seen the pumping station, which is able to lift three million gallons a day over a 1,000 ft hill to augment the water in the West Baldwin reservoir (see Route 10), from which supplies of water for Douglas and the south of the Island are drawn.

Tholt e Will Glen is heavily wooded and there is a pleasant waterfall about midway down it. The vegetation is very lush and a home for many birds.

### Refreshments

The Tholt e Will Country Inn provides snacks and drinks. It also has toilets.

### Public transport

None.

# Route 14

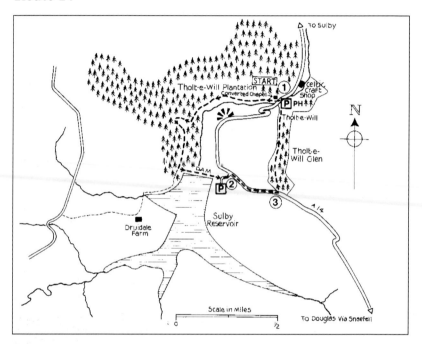

# ROUTE 14                               2 miles
## Sulby

**Start**

*At the Tholt e Will road bridge, OS Sheet 95 (GR 378897). Free car park adjacent to Celtic Crafts shop.*

**Route**

*1. A farm track begins near a small building which is a converted chapel with the year 1873 on its gable. It leads up the valley between the Sulby River and Sulby Plantation. The latter covers all the steeply sloping sides of the valley to the right of the track. Within half a mile, the track passes an attractive property with a bell tower on its roof and shortly afterwards makes a sharp zigzag and climbs steeply. Soon after it levels out, it provides access to the road running across the top of the dam on the left. Cross the dam. (But before continuing the walk proper, a wander along the bank of the reservoir on the right makes a pleasant addition to the day's outing).*

*2. Climb the two flights of steps at the far end of the dam and take the road which joins the Tholt e Will to Douglas road (A14). Turn right and, after passing through a yellow-painted cattle grid, look out for the sign indicating the entrance to Tholt e Will Glen on the left.*

*3. The path down the glen forks, the right one leading past a pleasant waterfall. Both paths come together further down the glen and lead behind the Inn to a wooden footbridge over the Sulby River to the vicinity of the Celtic Crafts shop.*

*The Sulby Reservoir*

*Spooyt Vane Waterfall*

# ROUTE 15
## Glen Wyllin
4 miles

### Outline
Glen Wyllin - Cooil Dharry - Spooyt Vane - Glen Mooar - Glen Wyllin

### Summary
This is a fairly easy walk mainly on farm tracks and country lanes from Glen Wyllin, near the north-western small town of Kirk Michael, to one of the highest waterfalls in the Island, and then through one of the glens to return to Glen Wyllin by the beach. Walking boots should be worn.

### Attractions
The lower part of Glen Wyllin (Mill Glen) is popular for those who enjoy living under canvas during the summer months. The camp site is well organised and has washing and toilet facilities. There is a children's playground by the river which runs through the glen, and the beach and sea are at its far end. Two very tall stone pillars in the glen used at one time to support a bridge carrying the steam railway line between Peel and Ramsey.

Cooil Dharry (Oak Nook) is a heavily wooded glade, mainly of beech but some oak, with a pretty stream running through it. It is a nature reserve owned by the Manx Nature Conservation Trust.

An extraordinary barrow-like hill called *Cronk Urleigh* or *Urley* (Eagle's Hill) can be seen across the valley on the left soon after leaving Cooil Dharry. A northern Tynwald Court was held here in 1422. (The main Tynwald Court is at St Johns, seen and explained in Route 6).

Spooyt Vane (White Spout) is a superb waterfall just inside Glen Mooar (Big Glen). It drops in two stages into a pool surrounded by ferns and mosses. It is well worth the detour to walk to the foot of the fall.

Cabbal Pheric (Patrick's chapel) is an early Christian chapel, 8th/10th century, whose ruined boundary walls and priest cell are all that are now visible. Its remoteness must have made it a very lonely place for any who worshipped there. Glen Mooar is heavily wooded and a number of special shrubs and plants have been introduced which make it a very attractive spot, especially in the spring and summer. Two huge stone pillars duplicate those in Glen Wyllin and had the same purpose.

### Refreshments
There are shops in Kirk Michael, which is five minute's walk from Glen Wyllin and can be most easily reached by a footpath leading to it from out of the glen. They should be able to supply food and drinks. There is also The Mitre public house nearly opposite the bus stop at Station Road.

### Public transport
By bus: Douglas Bus Station, service Nos 5 & 6 via Peel. The Kirk Michael bus stop is at Station Road. Walk back along this busy road to the junction with Peel Road and the A3 (about 150 yards), turn down the Peel Road for 300 yards. Glen Wyllin is on either side of the road.

## Route 15

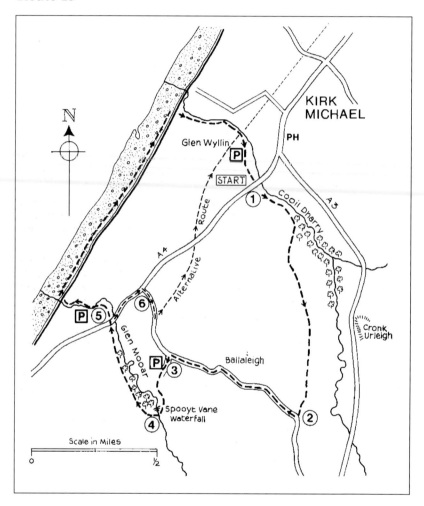

# ROUTE 15 4 miles
## Glen Wyllin

### Start

*Glen Wyllin is near Kirk Michael and is cut in two by the Kirk Michael to Peel road. The upper part of the glen is where the walk begins (OS Sheet 95, GR 314903). There is a free car park in the lower part of the glen. To reach the glen, take the A1 road from Douglas to Ballacraine Corner (just before St Johns and equipped with traffic lights). Turn right on to the A3 to Kirk Michael, take the first left after passing the town's 30mph sign and first right thereafter.*

### Route

1. *From the car park, return to and cross over the Peel Road. Soon after the last of the few cottages in this upper part of the glen have been left behind, a farm track replaces the metalled lane. Directly ahead is the nature reserve of Cooil Dharry, but the track turns to the right and uphill for just over quarter of a mile. As it flattens out, the wide valley on the left becomes visible and, on the far side of the major road which runs down it, the hill of Cronk Urleigh can be seen.*

2. *The track eventually becomes a surfaced country lane and joins a country road. Turn right at the junction, walking downhill. (The Mountains of Mourne and other parts of the northern Irish coast can sometimes be seen across the wide expanse of sea visible from this area).*

3. *When a small chapel, very overgrown with weeds and ivy, appears on the left, turn down the narrow lane beside it marked with a capital P and a capital T sign to indicate a car park and no through road. Passing the small car park, the lane becomes rough and often muddy. It leads to a footbridge over a stream.*

4. *Cross the bridge and turn right through a small wooden gate just beyond it. This gives access to Glen Mooar, the path to the Spooyt Vane waterfall being on the right. There are two main paths through the glen, but they join up lower down near two tall stone columns.*

5. *Cross the Peel/Kirk Michael road, following a continuation of the glen via a metalled lane. This leads to the beach. Turn right at the beach and walk along it to Glen Wyllin, which is roughly a mile away.*

6. *In bad weather or extreme spring tides, turn right upon reaching the Peel/Kirk Michael road and turn first right again. This leads to a disused railway track on the left, indicated by a green walker's sign. This will take you directly to Glen Wyllin. (See shorter route direction below).*

### Shorter route

*Should it be necessary to cut short this walk, do not turn left at the chapel, but continue along the road until the green footpath sign appears on the right. Turn right and follow the disused railway track leading directly to Glen Wyllin.*

*Ramsey harbour*

*Mooragh Park, Ramsey*

# ROUTE 16                   2.5 miles
## Ramsey

**Outline**

Grove Rural Life Museum - Mooragh Park - Ramsey Harbour - Grove Rural Life Museum

**Summary**

This short walk skirts the northern edge of Ramsey, the Island's second largest town, and then goes through the Mooragh Park and boating lake, across the harbour and, by way of a footpath beside the Sulby River, back to the Museum.

**Attractions**

The Grove Rural Life Museum is a time capsule Victorian period house which was originally developed as a summer retreat for a Victorian shipping merchant from Liverpool and his family. The rooms, from drawing room to scullery, retain their period furnishings augmented by displays of toys and costumes of the period.

The outbuildings house an interesting collection of vehicles and agricultural implements appropriate to the larger Manx farms of the 19th century. The four-horned Manx Loghtan sheep flock is often to be seen grazing nearby and the beautifully maintained gardens, complete with ducks and the odd Manx tail-less cat, are worth a visit. The conservatory with its colourful plants has been converted into a small cafe.

Mooragh Park was created about 100 years ago out of the Sulby River's old river bed and mud flats. With considerable ingenuity 40 acres were reclaimed and laid out with footpaths and gardens, sub-tropical plants helping to make it wonderfully colourful in summer. The many palm trees growing there add to its exotic appeal. There is a 12 acre lake for boats, a children's playground, two hard tennis courts, a bowling green, crazy golf, a café and a confectionery shop, both with toilets.

The tidal harbour is usually a hive of activity, with commercial coasters, yachts and trawlers to be seen. There is also a ship repair and building yard with often quite large vessels to be seen on the stocks. Near the southernmost of the harbour's two long breakwaters, there is a lifeboat station. The modern lifeboat is carried from its house across a road and launched over the sandy beach by means of a specially designed tractor.

**Refreshments**

Grove Rural Life Museum; Mooragh Park; West Quay Road. All supply refreshments.

**Public transport**

By bus: Douglas Bus Station, service No 15 or 15A to Ramsey Bus Station. Then service Nos 12, 17, 18, 19, 20 to Grove Rural Life Museum.

By electric train: Queens Promenade, Douglas Tramway terminus to Ramsey station. Then Ramsey Bus Station services above.

## Route 16

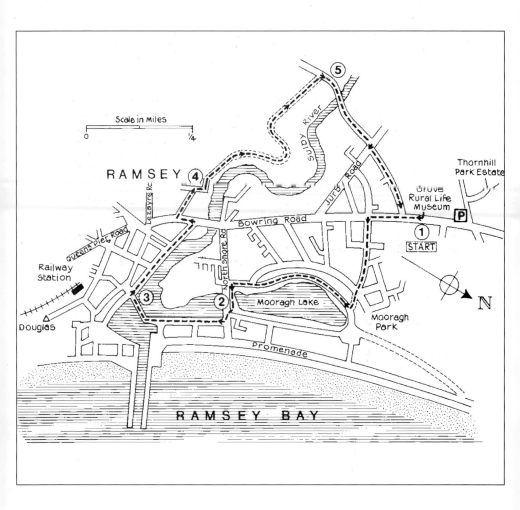